Collins

INTERNATIONAL
LOWER SECONDARY

T0340476

Computing
Workbook

8

Laura Sach

William Collins' dream of knowledge for all began with the publication of his first book in 1819.

A self-educated mill worker, he not only enriched millions of lives, but also founded a flourishing publishing house. Today, staying true to this spirit, Collins books are packed with inspiration, innovation and practical expertise.

They place you at the centre of a world of possibility and give you exactly what you need to explore it.

Collins. Freedom to teach.

Published by Collins

An imprint of HarperCollins*Publishers*
The News Building, 1 London Bridge Street, London,
SE1 9GF, UK

HarperCollins*Publishers*
Macken House, 39/40 Mayor Street Upper, Dublin 1,
D01 C9W8, Ireland

Browse the complete Collins catalogue at
collins.co.uk

© HarperCollins*Publishers* Limited 2024

10 9 8 7 6 5 4 3 2 1

ISBN 978-0-00-868406-8

British Library Cataloguing-in-Publication Data

A catalogue record for this publication is available from the British Library.

Author: Laura Sach
Publisher: Catherine Martin
Product manager: Saaleh Patel
Project manager: Just Content Ltd
Development editor: Julie Bond
Copy editor: Paul Clowrey
Proofreader: Laura Connell and Tanya Solomons
Cover designer: Gordon McGilp
Cover image: Amparo Barrera, Kneath Associates
Internal designer: Steve Evans, Planet Life Art
Illustrations: Jouve India Ltd
Typesetter: Ken Vail Graphic Design
Production controller: Lyndsey Rogers
Printed and bound by Martins the Printers

MIX
Paper | Supporting responsible forestry
FSC™ C007454

This book contains FSC™ certified paper and other controlled sources to ensure responsible forest management.

For more information visit: harpercollins.co.uk/green

Acknowledgements

The publishers gratefully acknowledge the permission granted to reproduce the copyright material in this book. Every effort has been made to trace copyright holders and to obtain their permission for the use of copyright material. The publishers will gladly receive any information enabling them to rectify any error or omission at the first opportunity.

Support materials and screenshots are licensed under the Creative Commons Attribution-ShareAlike 2.0 license. We are grateful to the following for permission to reproduce screenshots. In some instances, we have been unable to trace the owners of copyright material, and we would appreciate any information that would enable us to do so.

Python Software Foundation: Permission obtained to use screenshots demonstrating Python programming language features.

Scratch Foundation: Authorised usage of screenshots showcasing Scratch programming environment elements.

EduBlocks: Granted clearance for the inclusion of screenshots depicting EduBlocks interface and functionalities.

Scratch is developed by the Lifelong Kindergarten Group at the MIT Media Lab: p.30, p.31, p.39.

PSF's License Agreement and PSF's notice of copyright, i.e., "Copyright (c) 2001 Python Software Foundation; All Rights Reserved" are retained in Python 2.0.1 alone or in any derivative version prepared by Collins (Licensee): p.30, p.38–39, p.60, p.69.

Images

p.35 Kid_Games_Catalog/Shutterstock, p.37 KARTHIKEYAN_R/Shutterstock, p.45 Luba_nn/Shutterstock, p.48 Frogella/Shutterstock.

Contents

Introduction

The Collins Stage 8 Student's Book and Workbook offer a rich programme of skills development, based on a varied and stimulating set of projects grounded in real-world contexts.

The Stage 8 Workbook directly supports the Student's Book, with Workbook tasks for every lesson in the Student's Book. The Workbook tasks are clearly referenced in the Student's Book to make the link between the two resources clear.

Each task provides the context and scaffolding required to complete any paper-based tasks during a lesson. This allows you to build a record of your notes and designs that are separate to the work you create using software. You can use the Workbook to remind yourself about plans and designs you have created and concepts you have learned about.

Regular reflection tasks are included in which you have an opportunity to privately consider your thoughts about a particular lesson or a skill you have been practising. These can be shared with the class if there is an opportunity or kept private between you and your teacher.

Each lesson ends with an optional homework task in the Workbook which your teacher may set to help you consolidate what you have learned during the lesson, or research something new to enhance your learning about the topic.

I hope my approach helps you and your teachers to enjoy learning about computing, digital literacy and ICT in a practical and enjoyable way.

Laura Sach

Chapter 1 — Our digital world

Project: Targeted advertisement

Chapter 1.1 Evaluating online information

Task A. Evaluate the URL

What can you tell about these websites just from looking at the URL at the top of the web browser?

Website	Comments
Visit the online encyclopedia, Wikipedia.	
Visit the YouTube website.	
Visit the home page of Canada.	

Key terms

Advertisement – a notice telling people about a product

AI image generator – a piece of software that uses artificial intelligence to generate images based on a text description typed in by the user

Cookie – a small amount of data stored on your computer by a website

Data mining – analysing large amounts of data to find patterns and trends

IP address – an address allocated to you by your internet service provider, which reveals your rough geographical location. An IP address looks like a set of four numbers separated with a dot, for example 172.217.22.14

Metadata – 'data about data', for example who created the data, when it was created, and what device it was created on

Model – a simulation of a real-life system on a computer

Uniform Resource Locator (URL) – a unique address that specifies the location of a website

'What if' scenario – a simulation involving a set of criteria being applied to a model, so that the result can be observed

Return to page 3 of the Student's Book.

Task B. Mind map

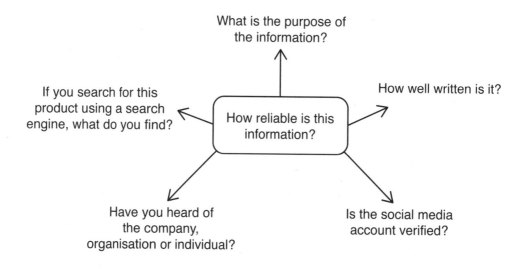

Figure 1.1.1 Judging online content – mind map.

You are looking at a social media post – this could be text, an image or a video – written by someone you do not know. There are several questions you can ask yourself to work out whether the information in the post is reliable or not.

1 For each question on the mind map, add a potential answer, if appropriate, or a comment on the type of answer, you would expect if the information was reliable.

2 Think of two more questions you could ask to evaluate the reliability of information from social media and add them to the diagram.

Return to page 3 of the Student's Book.

Reflection

What did you learn during this lesson that you had not thought about before?

....

....

Which do you think is the most important indicator of whether a source of online information is reliable or not, and why?

....

....

Homework

Choose another source of information found online – this could be a whole webpage or one part of a page, such as an advertisement, an email or a social media post.

Explain, showing examples from the source, how you can tell whether the information is reliable. You can draw or stick in parts of the source to help you to explain your answer if you wish.

Chapter 1.2 Usernames and metadata

Task A. Why choose an anonymous username?

Why should your username not reveal your personal identity? Write one reason in each of the boxes.

Return to page 4 of the Student's Book.

Task B. What metadata is recorded?

For each of these actions, write down the metadata that might be recorded about you. The first row has been filled in as an example.

Action	Metadata
Visit an online shopping website	• Time and date you visited the website • The device you were using • Items you looked at • Items you added to your cart • What you typed in the search box
Search for a route between your house and a relative's house using an online map	
Look at a website about a holiday destination	
Look at your favourite celebrity's or sports team's social media page	

Return to page 5 of the Student's Book.

Task C. Data from cookies

Use this space to note down any interesting data you find stored in cookies.

Return to page 6 of the Student's Book.

Reflection

Are you concerned about anything you learned today?

....

....

Will you change anything about the way you use the internet as a result of this lesson?

....

....

Homework

Here is some metadata about the user of a website. Write down the information you can deduce about this person from the metadata.

```
CurrencySelection: last_modified=27/10/2023+13:52:57&currency=USD
GlobalE_Data: {"CountryISO":"US","Language":"en-us"}
UserInfo: {"username":"brooke12",signInType:"PUBLIC","password":"r3f-
wed78f32hfg21ujt32wtg32fvdwsg2378fy389y32t4bh12efe"}
RETURNING_VISITOR: True
GeoIPloc:"US:NY:Long Island"
```

....

....

....

....

....

Chapter 1.3 Data mining

Task A. Why is metadata useful?

For each item of metadata, describe what information the data provides, and why that would be useful to a company. An example has been completed for you.

Metadata	Why is it useful to a company?
Device used to visit the page	If the customer is using an expensive device, this could reveal information about their income.
Date and time of user visit(s)	
Which pages were visited	
Words typed in a search box	
IP address	

Return to page 8 of the Student's Book.

Task B. Interrogate the data

Use the data provided to answer the following questions:

1 Which page was the first one visited on the 8th May 2023? ....

2 How many times did users search on the website? ....

3 How long was the longest visit? ....

4 Which page was the most popular in terms of visits? ....

5 What was the mean average number of seconds per visit? ....

6 How many different people added an item to their cart? ....

7 Which country visited the site the most? ....

8 Using the spreadsheet software, draw a bar chart of the number of searches done by people from each country. Remember to label the axes and give your chart a title.

Return to page 10 of the Student's Book.

Reflection

Mark on the scale how confident you feel that you can explain what metadata is, and what it is used for, to another person.

Completely confident _____ Not at all confident

Which part of the three lessons on this topic so far have you enjoyed the most, and why?

....

....

Homework

Why is it difficult to determine which item was the most searched for?

....

....

Can you come up with an idea for how you could measure which item was the most searched for, using the data available?

....

....

Chapter 1.4 Models

Task A. New lunch product

Decide on a lunch product, aimed at people of your age. Follow the checklist to create a model of the costs involved in creating the product. Tick off each instruction as you complete it.

> **Tip** If you are struggling for inspiration for a product, try browsing a recipe website. To find the prices of ingredients, you could look at a grocery website.

Data

☐ Decide on a lunch product.

☐ Write down all of the **ingredients** on the spreadsheet under Option 1. Add more rows if needed.

☐ Search online to look up the **pack cost** of each item that will go into your product. For example, if your product contains rice, look up how much a whole packet of rice is.

☐ Look up or estimate how many **servings are in the pack**.

☐ Divide the pack cost by the number of servings to get the **portion cost** for that ingredient.

☐ Add the pack cost, servings in pack and portion cost for *all* of the ingredients.

Formulae

☐ Calculate the **total cost** of all of the ingredients.

☐ Decide what **price** you would like to sell one portion for and type it in the box. (You cannot sell the product for less than you paid for the ingredients.)

☐ Calculate the **overall cost** – this is the amount you will need to pay for one portion, multiplied by the number sold.

☐ Calculate the **revenue** – this is the price of the product multiplied by the number sold.

☐ Calculate the **profit** – this is the revenue minus the overall cost.

Formatting

☐ Use conditional formatting to colour cell B8 differently depending on whether you made a profit (the number is greater than 0) or a loss (the number is less than 0).

☐ Format all of the cells that contain currency values with the correct currency format.

☐ Format all of the cells that contain whole numbers with a whole number format (with no decimal places).

Return to page 13 of the Student's Book.

Reflection

How well do you think you did at remembering how to use the spreadsheet skills you had already learned in a previous stage?

....

....

Was there anything that didn't go well when creating your model?

....

What spreadsheet skills do you think you need to improve on, and why?

....

....

Homework

Is there any data missing from your model? Write down any extra data you would need to consider if you were actually making this product in real life. Asking an adult at home with any experience of running a business would be useful.

....

....

....

....

....

....

Chapter 1.5 Create an advert

Task A. Draw a design for your advert

Draw a design for your advertisement. Remember to include the **price** you decided to charge for the product when you created your spreadsheet model.

Return to page 14 of the Student's Book.

Reflection

What do you think will be the most effective feature of your advert to attract your classmates to buy your food?

....

....

Is there anything you would have done differently if you started this task again? How would you do it differently?

....

....

Homework

During this lesson you used an AI image generator.

1 Explain two ways in which this technology could benefit people.

....

....

....

....

2 Explain two ways in which this technology might cause problems or not be beneficial.

....

....

....

....

Chapter 1.6 'What if' analysis

Task A. What if scenarios

Model the following scenarios on your spreadsheet.

- For each scenario, save a separate copy of your model before you begin.
- Your teacher will tell you the missing values to write in the gaps.

1 Your .... has broken and you need to buy a new one!

This will add a one-off amount of .... to your costs.

What did you change to model this scenario?

....

....

What is the *result* of this change on your profit, if you still sell 10 products?

....

....

How many of your products do you now need to sell to cover your costs?

....

2 What if the price of all vegetables goes up by 10%?
(Hint: To increase by 10%, multiply the current cost by 1.1.)

What did you change to model this scenario?

....

....

What is the *result* of this change on your profit if you still sell 10 products?

....

....

How many of your products do you now need to sell to cover your costs?

....

Return to page 18 of the Student's Book.

Reflection

Did your business idea make a profit?

....

Why do you think you did or did not make a profit?

....

....

Do you think that the model was helpful when making your decisions about what to change? Why, or why not?

....

....

Homework

Here are some real costs from a bakery spreadsheet model. Use this data to answer the questions. Assume that all the numbers have been rounded up to two decimal places.

	A	B	C	D	E	F
1	Product	Cost of recipe	Quantity made	How many in pack	Packaging price	Pack cost price
2	Brownie	2.47	8	2	0.04	0.66
3	Banana loaf	1.73	2	1	0.08	0.94
4	Dark chocolate cookie	3.50	12	3	0.04	0.92
5	Samosa	7.70	12	1	0.04	0.68
6	Cheese biscuits	2.37	24	4	0.08	0.47

1 What formula would the bakery use to calculate the **pack cost price** of the cheese biscuits?

....

2 Bags and boxes both cost 0.04 each. Which bakery items need both a bag and a box? Explain how you know the answer.

....

3 What if the baker has an accident and drops two brownies on the floor, meaning they cannot be sold. Write down which cell in the model you would change, and the new value.

....

4 What would be the effect on the pack cost price of the baker dropping two brownies?

....

5 The baker realises that the cookies need a bag *and* a box, so she changes the formula for the **pack cost price** of dark chocolate cookies to the following formula:

=((B4/C4)*D4)+0.08

Explain what is wrong with the change she has made, and what she should have done instead.

....

....

....

Assessment checklist

- ☐ I know three questions I can ask to evaluate the reliability of information online.
- ☐ I can explain to a friend what a URL is.
- ☐ I can use a URL to deduce information about a website.
- ☐ I can give two reasons why my username should not reveal my personal identity.
- ☐ I can explain to a friend what metadata is.
- ☐ I can give four examples of metadata which might be collected when I visit a website.
- ☐ I have looked at the contents of a cookie in my browser.
- ☐ I know what an IP address is and how to find my public IP address.
- ☐ I can sort data in a spreadsheet.
- ☐ I can calculate the mean average of data in a spreadsheet.
- ☐ I can draw a meaningful graph of data from a spreadsheet.
- ☐ I can write a prompt to generate the image I want from an AI image generator.
- ☐ I know what a data model is and why it is useful.
- ☐ I can build a data model using a spreadsheet.
- ☐ I can ask a 'what if' question and simulate the results using a spreadsheet.
- ☐ I can make changes to a model to achieve a particular goal (e.g. not making a loss).

Chapter 2 Content creation
Project: Virtual tour

Chapter 2.1 Know your audience

Task A. Features of a virtual tour

What could each of these be used for in a virtual tour?

Images	
Text	
Video	
Sound	
Buttons	
Maps	

Return to page 22 of the Student's Book.

Task B. When is it appropriate?

Add a tick (✓) to the table to show when it is appropriate to use emojis, GIFs and memes. Think about the context as well as the format of the communication when you answer.

Situation	Emoji	Meme	GIF
An instant message to a friend			
An instant message to a grandparent			
A social media post			
An invitation to a party			
A History assignment for school			
An article for the school newspaper			

Were there any situations where you were not sure? Why?

....

....

Return to page 24 of the Student's Book.

Key terms

Audience – the people who will look at the work you produce

Augmented reality – using technology to superimpose digital content on top of a real-world environment

Emoji – a small icon used in text to express an emotion or represent an item

GIF – an image format that allows animation

Hotspot – an area on the screen that the user can click on to perform an action

Meme – a familiar image, often accompanied with text, which is shared and reused on the internet

Multimedia – using more than one method of presenting information, e.g. text, images, sound and/or video

Navigation – the way a user moves through a presentation or a website

Search term – the text you write into a search engine to find what you need

Template – a pre-designed format for a document

Virtual tour – a simulation of being at a particular location, involving multimedia such as images, text and perhaps also sound and video

Task C. Plan your virtual tour

Use this space to plan your virtual tour with your partner. You should plan to visit four different locations as part of your tour. Think about the key pieces of information you want to communicate for each location and what media (e.g. images, sound, video) you plan to use for each location.

Virtual tour of: ....

Audience: ....

Part of the tour	Key information	Media

Return to page 24 of the Student's Book.

Reflection

Do you use emojis, gifs or memes? What do you think they add to a conversation that text cannot provide?

....

....

The way people communicate has changed since you were born. Do you think this is a good thing or a bad thing?

....

....

Homework

Find a real example of communication (e.g. an advert, a menu, a newspaper article, a social media post) and analyse whether the communication is appropriate for the audience.

Chapter 2.2 Document templates

Task A. What are the benefits of using a document template?

Match the features of a document template with their benefits by drawing a line between each pair of statements.

The template style is automatically applied to the whole document

Allows anyone to create a document that looks good

You can use a template that someone else has designed

The document always looks professional

Styles are the same everywhere they are used

If you need to change something, you only need to change it once in the template

Documents can be set up to match a company's branding

The document looks consistent

Return to page 27 of the Student's Book.

Task B. Draw your template design

Draw and annotate the features of your template design idea in the box below. Make sure to think about:

- fonts, sizes and colours
- where images will be placed, and how big they will be.

Return to page 27 of the Student's Book.

Reflection

What features of your template make it suitable for the audience you have chosen for your virtual tour?

....

....

....

Are there any features you are not sure about, and why?

....

....

Do you think that using a template is a good way of working? Why, or why not?

....

....

Homework

Find an example of a real-life document. Draw a design for a template that could be used to improve the document.

Chapter 2.3 Searching for information

Task A. What extra information do you need?

What extra information do you need to complete your tour, and where might you find this information? An example is given in the top row to show you some information someone might want to collect if they were creating a virtual tour of their school.

Tour page	Extra information needed	Where will I find it?
Front of main school building	What date was the school built? Who were the founders?	School website Local history website about my town

Return to page 29 of the Student's Book.

Task B. Web quest

A web quest is where you use a search engine to find pieces of information. Use your favourite search engine to search for the answers to these questions.

What sweet treat is the city of Bath, UK, famous for?	Find out the name of a famous singer or band from your local area. ....
What is the cheapest price you can find for a cardboard cake box?	Find a golf club that is near a wood or forest. ....

Return to page 30 of the Student's Book.

Reflection

Did you have any problems when you were searching for information on the internet? What were they?

....

....

How effective were the skills you learned this lesson at improving your searches?

....

....

Homework

Research an additional piece of information for your virtual tour – this could be in any format, e.g. text or a digital image. Bring the information to the next lesson and add it to your virtual tour. A space is provided below if you need to make notes.

Chapter 2.4 Using multimedia

Task A. What is it used for?

Which type(s) of media would you choose for each of these scenarios, and why?

An interview with the author of a children's book

....

A recipe

....

A catalogue for the products a business sells

....

A tutorial explaining how to make something

....

Return to page 31 of the Student's Book.

Task B. Class guidelines for safe use of multimedia devices

Write down the guidelines your class has agreed on for using technology safely.

- ....
  ....

- ....
  ....

- ....
  ....

- ....
  ....

- ....
  ....

Return to page 32 of the Student's Book.

Reflection

How confident did you feel about collecting material using different types of media? Were you any more or less confident with any in particular?

....

....

....

Homework

Think about each of the following situations where multimedia devices are being used. What could go wrong, and are there any precautions you could take to make sure everyone stays safe?

Scenario	What could go wrong?	Precautions to take
1 You are recording a video for a virtual tour of your school. During the recording, a teacher of another subject walks past with their class.		
2 You are taking photographs to use in your tour. Your partner takes a photograph on their mobile phone of you in a room that is part of the tour.		
3 You are recording a video of yourself visiting a local landmark as part of your virtual tour. Your partner wants to see the video and suggests that you upload it onto a video streaming site so that they can see it.		

Chapter 2.5 Presentation software

Task A. Navigation

How will your user navigate through your virtual tour? Draw a diagram to show which parts of the tour will link to which other parts. Will you have a map allowing the user to choose where they go?

Return to page 33 of the Student's Book.

Reflection

What have you enjoyed about working with a partner on this task?

....

....

Was there anything you found frustrating about working with a partner?
What would you do to avoid this next time you are working in pairs?

....

....

Do you think your partner found anything frustrating about working with you?
How would you change your approach the next time you are working in pairs?

....

....

....

Homework

Making something *accessible* means designing it so that it can be used successfully by a person with a disability. Research and write down some advice you would give on the following topics to make sure that your virtual tour is accessible to as many people as possible.

Accessibility topic	Advice
Size of buttons	
Text contrast	
Colour choice	
Font choice	

Chapter 2.6 Augmented reality

Task A. What are the benefits and drawbacks of augmented reality?

What are the benefits and drawbacks of augmented reality apps in the following situations? Try to write *two* points in each box.

	Benefits	**Drawbacks**
Education		
Entertainment		

Return to page 36 of the Student's Book.

Reflection

Did you win any awards? Which award are you most proud of?

....

....

If you had more time, what would you improve about your tour?

....

....

Homework

If you could use augmented reality technology, how would you use it to enhance a *real-life* tour of a place? This does not have to be the same place you focused on for your virtual tour.

What benefits would augmented reality add for visitors taking the tour? Sketch an idea and write down some notes about how it would work.

....

....

....

....

....

Assessment checklist

- ☐ I can describe the features of a virtual tour.
- ☐ I can explain when it is appropriate to use communication devices such as emojis, GIFs and memes.
- ☐ I can create a document template for a presentation document.
- ☐ I can explain the benefits of using a document template.
- ☐ I can type confidently and at a reasonable speed.
- ☐ I can deliberately exclude or require certain terms to be part of a search performed using a search engine.
- ☐ I can collaborate with a partner on a project, dividing the work fairly.
- ☐ I can use a multimedia device, such as a camera or microphone, to collect information.
- ☐ I know how to keep myself and my friends safe when using multimedia devices, such as tablets and mobile phones.
- ☐ I can combine text, images and other media to create a presentation.
- ☐ I can link from a slide to other slides in a presentation.
- ☐ I know what is meant by augmented reality.
- ☐ I can list some uses of augmented reality.

Chapter 3 — Create with code 1

Project: Fantasy name generator

Chapter 3.1 Familiarisation with Python

Task A. Writing a Python program

Fill in the table below to remind you how to open your Python development environment and run a program. You could write instructions for yourself or draw a sketch if that helps.

Task	How do I do it?
Open the Python development environment	
Write the following program: `print("Hello world")`	
Save the program	
Run the program	

Return to page 40 of the Student's Book.

Task B. Recreate the Scratch program

Write down the Python code you would use to recreate the Scratch program in Python

Scratch	Python
Figure 3.1.1 Scratch name input and output program.	

Key terms

Code review – a software developer checking code written by another developer and suggesting improvements

Comment – a note written for a human to read in a program. All comments are completely ignored by the computer

Concatenation – joining two or more pieces of text together

Constant – a value that does not change while the program is running

Decomposition – the process of breaking down a complex problem into smaller, more manageable tasks

Iterative development – regularly adding new features and improvements to a piece of software, and then seeking feedback to inform the next set of improvements

List – a data structure that can hold more than one piece of data

Program library – a collection of pre-written code that can be imported and used within another program

Random – chosen by chance

String – a sequence of letters, numbers and/or punctuation, usually written within quotation marks

Text-based language – allows you to type text instructions that a computer can run

User feedback – feedback from a person who uses a piece of software

Now type your Python code into a program and run it to check whether you were right.

Did your code do what you predicted it would do? If not, what was different?

....

....

Return to page 41 of the Student's Book.

Reflection

What differences did you spot between Python and Scratch?

....

....

....

Which do you prefer using, and why?

....

....

....

Homework

What would be the output of each of these programs, assuming the values of variables given in the table? Take extra care to notice where there are (or are not) spaces within the strings.

Variable	Value
name	Maryam
subject	Science
colour	blue

```
print(name + " likes " + subject)
```

....

```
print(subject + " is " + name + "'s favourite subject")
```

....

```
print("I like blue. " + name + " likes " + colour)
```

....

```
print("Favourites: " + subject + ", " + colour)
```

....

```
print("Maryam's clothes are" + colour)
```

....

Chapter 3.2 Program library

Task A. Video game program library

Write down five ideas for pre-written functions that a program library for creating video games might have. An example has been given to get you started.

1 Function to move a character left and right

2 ....

3 ....

4 ....

5 ....

6 ....

Return to page 44 of the Student's Book.

Task B. Guess what this code does

Look at this program:

```
import random
print( random.randint(1, 6) )
```

Write down what you think the output of this program will be when it is run.

....

Type in and run the program. Did you get the output you predicted? If not, what output did you get?

....

Run the program a few more times, then explain in your own words what this program does.

....

....

Return to page 45 of the Student's Book.

Reflection

What programming technique from this lesson do you think will be the most useful to use again in a future program, and why?

....

....

Which part of this lesson did you find the most difficult, and why?

....

....

....

Homework

Describe the purpose of a program library

....

....

....

You have used the random library to generate random integer numbers with randint() and random choices from a list with choice().

Write a tick (✓) if the variable result could have that value, or a cross (✗) if it is not possible. An example has been done for you.

Code	Value	Possible?
`import random` `result = random.randint(1, 10)`	1	✓
	6	
	0	
	1.5	

`import random`
`result = random.choice(["apple", "pear",`
`"orange", "banana"])`
	"pear"	

	"kiwi"	
	"choice"	

Chapter 3.3 Decomposition

Task A. Decompose a game

Think of a game that you are familiar with. In each box, draw or write how you would break the game down into smaller parts to explain the rules to a friend.

Return to page 48 of the Student's Book.

Task B. What's in a name?

Look at the example names you have been given:

- Fearless Nazir, musician of Lavaland
- Cheerful Asma, builder of Azimuth

A name has been broken up into four parts. Underneath each part, give a description of what that part represents. For example, the first part of each name is always an adjective (a describing word).

Fearless	Nazir	musician	of Lavaland
An adjective			

Return to page 49 of the Student's Book.

Reflection

Write down two ways that using decomposition helped you to plan your program.

....

....

Did you find anything about the decomposition process unhelpful?

....

Would you use decomposition again when planning a program? Why, or why not?

....

Homework

Drawing a particular object is often broken up into step-by-step instructions for beginners.

Decompose something you know how to draw into steps, as in the example shown here.

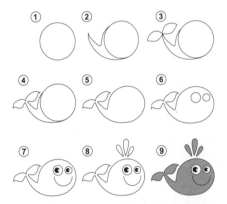

Figure 3.3.1 Drawing a cartoon whale in stages.

Chapter 3.4 Name generator

Task A. Constants

Fill in the missing words in the gaps below to describe three benefits of using constants. You do not need to use all the words, so choose carefully!

uppercase	end	does not	one	start	price
value	0.8	every	does	lowercase	name

A constant is defined in one place, usually at the .... of the program. If you need to change the value of the constant in the code, you need to find and replace .... value to update the whole program.

Constants are clearly distinguished from variables by putting their names in .... The .... of the constant is then used in the code instead of its .... Anyone reading the program has a clear indication of what the constant represents.

Here is some code that .... use a constant.

```
total = price * 0.8
```

You could use a constant called DISCOUNT to hold the value ...., which would make the meaning of the code much clearer.

Return to page 52 of the Student's Book.

Reflection

What did you find easy when translating your flowchart into real program code?

....

....

Did you write all of your program at once, or did you write part of the program and then test it? Do you think your method worked well?

....

....

If you could time travel, what advice would you have given yourself at the start of the lesson?

....

....

Homework

This program uses the random library to simulate flipping this coin.

Figure 3.4.1 Flipping a coin.

Add a comment at each position marked with a # to explain what is happening in the following line(s) of code:

```python
import random

# .............................................................................................
GAZELLE = 1
WRITING = 0

# .............................................................................................
SIDES = [GAZELLE, WRITING]

# .............................................................................................

# .............................................................................................
coin1 = random.choice(SIDES)
coin2 = random.choice(SIDES)
coin3 = random.choice(SIDES)
coin4 = random.choice(SIDES)
coin5 = random.choice(SIDES)

# .............................................................................................
total = coin1 + coin2 + coin3 + coin4 + coin5
#
total = str(total)

# .............................................................................................
print("You got " + total + " gazelles")
```

Chapter 3.5 Story generator

Task A. Design your story

Note down some new ideas you could randomly generate to create a story. These could be items, describing words, places, things the character might say: the choice is up to you.

An example has been given, but you don't have to use it in your story if you don't want to.

Idea	Possible values
Quest item	special crystal, golden stone, power stone

Return to page 53 of the Student's Book.

Task B. What does the error message mean?

Here are some examples of error messages you might see in Python. Write down under each one what the error message means and what you should do to solve it.

```
print( name + " decided to leave " + plac)
```

Python error: NameError: name 'plac' is not defined.

....

....

```
print(name   " was fed up with being a "   + job)
```

Python error: Invalid syntax

....

....

```
print("He had a quest to find a " + item)
```

Python error: TypeError: can only concatenate str (not "list") to str

....

....

Return to page 54 of the Student's Book.

Reflection

Is there anything you would like to add to your story but you don't know how to do?

....

....

....

Based on your experience with other programming languages such as Scratch, which features of Python do you think you might need to learn about so you can add these new parts to your story?

....

....

....

Homework

Here is a piece of code. It has five bugs. Highlight each piece of code that would cause a bug and annotate what you would do to fix it.

```
import random
ADJECTIVES = ["fearless", "cheerful", "friendly")
place = random.choice(PLACES)
PLACES = ["Lavaland", "Azimuth", "Coalville"]
ENEMIES = ["mammoth", "giant spider", "large sheep"]
name = input("Please type in your name: ")
description = random.randint(ADJECTIVES)
enemy = random.choice(ENEMIES)
print("There was once a " + description + " person called " name)
print("One day, a " + enemy + " came to " + place)
```

Chapter 3.6 Feedback on software

Task A. Code review focus

In the left-hand column of this table, write down four things that you would like your code reviewer to provide written feedback on when they do a code review. (Do not fill in the right-hand column yet.)

Area to look at	Could be better if...

Return to page 55 of the Student's Book.

Task B. Review the code

You are the code reviewer. Look at your partner's code and, for each row in the table, write down a way that your partner could improve their code.

Tip	Remember to make your comment as helpful as possible. For example, "You could use constants for the lists called job and place" is better than "You forgot to use constants".

Return to page 55 of the Student's Book.

Task C. User feedback focus

Write down four things that you would like your user to provide written feedback on in the left-hand column of this table. (Do not fill in the right-hand column yet.)

Comment on	Could be better if...

Return to page 56 of the Student's Book.

Task D. Give user feedback

You are the user. Look at your partner's program when it is running, and for each row in the table write down a way in which your partner could improve their program.

> **Tip** Remember that you are *not* looking at the code, only the output of the program on the screen.

Return to page 56 of the Student's Book.

Reflection

Giving good feedback

Which one piece of feedback did you find the most helpful? Explain why this feedback was helpful.

....

....

....

Did you receive any feedback you found unhelpful? Explain why it was unhelpful.

....

....

....

Homework

In this lesson, you used **iterative development** to improve your code after receiving feedback. Research and write down in your own words what the word 'iterative' means, in terms of developing a piece of software.

....

....

One reason to do a **code review** is so that a new piece of code can be checked by someone else for bugs. Give two other reasons why software developers review each other's code.

....

....

Sometimes developers collect **user feedback** by asking the user what they think, like you did during this lesson. Sometimes, a software developer watches a user as they use the software to complete a task, without speaking to them. Explain how watching the user would provide useful feedback for the software developer.

....

....

Assessment checklist

☐ I know how to create and save a new Python program.

☐ I can write a Python program that has an output (print).

☐ I can write a Python program that has an input.

☐ I know how to create a variable in Python and assign it a value.

☐ I can describe what a program library is and what it is used for.

☐ I can use a function from a program library (for example, random.choice()).

☐ I can think about a problem and break it down into smaller problems.

☐ I can draw a flowchart to plan a piece of code.

☐ I can describe the purpose of a constant, and I know how to use one in a program.

☐ I can use a flowchart to help me write the same algorithm in code.

☐ I can use comments in a program, and I know why they are useful.

☐ I can work on a program iteratively, adding new features bit by bit.

☐ I can perform a code review on some code written by someone else.

☐ I can provide helpful feedback to someone else about their program.

☐ I can use feedback from someone else to make improvements to my own code.

Chapter 4 | How computers work

Project: Troubleshooter

Key terms

Application software – allows the computer user to do a task, for example a web browser or a word processor

Compression – significantly reducing the amount of storage space a file requires

Driver – a small piece of software that allows the operating system to communicate with a hardware device such as a printer

Ethernet cable – a type of network cable used to connect computers and other network devices such as routers together

File access permissions – restrict access to files and folders on a network to only the people who need to see them

Firewall – provides a layer of protection between two networks, preventing threats from entering, and sensitive information from leaving

Internet of Things (IoT) – a network of interconnected devices, appliances and physical objects, typically containing sensors, which communicate across the internet

Malware – **mal**icious soft**ware**. Any software that intends to cause harm to a computer, for example a virus

Network – a collection of computers that are connected together to exchange data

Operating system (OS) – an important piece of software that manages all other software and hardware devices

Port – a number assigned to each type of network traffic going in or out of a firewall

---

Chapter 4.1 Memory

Task A. Classify the animals

Use the flowchart to correctly classify the following animals: cat, snake, spider, worm.

Write the name of each animal in the correct box.

> Figure 4.1.1 Animal classification flowchart.

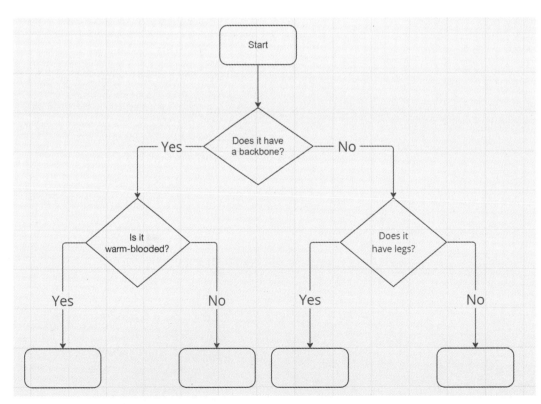

Return to page 59 of the Student's Book.

Key terms

RAM – Random Access Memory, used to store instructions and data the computer is currently working with. Contents are lost when the power is switched off

ROM – Read Only Memory, stores the instructions needed to load the operating system. Contents are kept when the power is switched off

Router – a networking device that connects two or more networks together

Scheduling – a task performed by the operating system to make sure each piece of software gets a turn to use the processor

Troubleshooter – a tool or guide that gathers information to pinpoint the cause of a problem, and then offers advice on how to fix it

Utility software – keeps the computer secure and in working order, for example antivirus software

Wired network – computers and network devices connected using physical cables such as ethernet cables

Wireless network – computers and network devices that connect and communicate via radio signals

Task B. Memory role play

Before you start the activity, colour in each number with a different coloured pencil to make a key.

1	2	3	4	5

Your teacher will explain how to do the activity. Colour the picture according to the instructions given to you by your partner.

Return to page 61 of the Student's Book.

Reflection

What have you learned today that you did not know before?

....

....

Did you have any problems with starting to create the troubleshooter?

....

....

What will you do in the next lesson to help resolve the problem(s)?

....

....

Homework

Find out the specification of a computer – this could be a computer you own, or your dream computer that you would like to buy.

How much RAM does it have? ....

How much secondary storage does it have? ....

How many times larger is the secondary storage than the RAM? (Tip: If both are measured in GB, you can divide the secondary storage by the RAM to find out!)

....

Chapter 4.2 The operating system

Task A. Which tasks are performed by the operating system?

Which tasks are performed by the operating system? Sort the statements into two categories – Tasks done by the OS, and Tasks not done by the OS.

> **Tip** Complete the key by filling in a colour or designing a symbol for each category. Then use the correct colour or symbol next to each statement in the table.

Key:

Task done by the OS		Task not done by the OS	

Plays music		Protects the computer against viruses	
Allocates the system's memory		Allocates processing time	
Displays your files so that you can find and access them		Lets you play a video game	
Records a voice note		Provides software to create a presentation	
Stores the instructions required to start up the computer		Communicates with hardware devices	

Return to page 64 of the Student's Book.

Task B. Troubleshooter problems

Problems with the operation of your computer can often be resolved using features of the operating system. Look at the questions in the table and think about what could be causing each problem, and what question you would need to ask next in the troubleshooter to get more information.

An example has been filled in to show you.

Question	If no, possible causes	Next question
Is your computer starting up?	• Not plugged in • Problem loading the operating system	• Is your computer plugged in and switched on? • Can you see the operating system's logo or any text on the screen?
Is your printer working correctly?		
Can you find the file you need?		
Is your keyboard working?		

Return to page 65 of the Student's Book.

Reflection

How confident are you on a scale of 1–10 (10 being totally confident) that you know which tasks are handled by the operating system? Why did you give this score?

....

Was there anything in this lesson you were unsure about?

....

....

Homework

Look at the image. Which tasks are handled by the operating system, and which would be handled by application software?

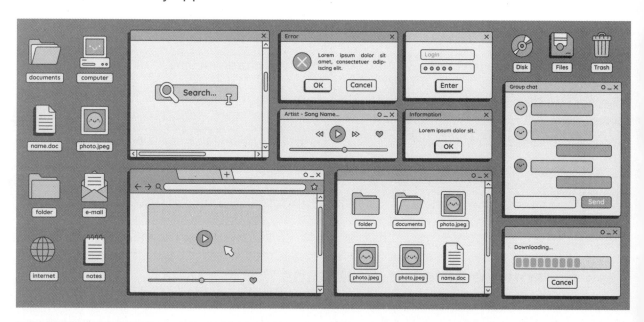

Operating system	Application software

Chapter 4.3 Utility programs

Task A. Purpose of utility programs

Draw lines to match each task to the utility program that performs it.

- Move a file from one location to another   Anti-malware software

- Detect and remove a virus

- Backup a folder   Backup software

- Find a specific file

- Reduce the amount of storage space a
  file requires   File manager

- Scan an email attachment to check that
  it is safe to open   Compression software

Return to page 66 of the Student's Book.

Task B. Advice from a technician

You are a network IT technician in a large company. Reply with some advice to the
following people who have sent you a message:

1 Masood says: "Hi! I have received an email from my boss with a customer list
attached. I didn't ask him to send me this list so I am a bit worried it might be
a virus."

....

....

2 Amara says: "My computer is showing an odd message saying I have to pay
money to release my files. Help!"

....

....

3 Miguel says "I would like to know what precautions the IT support department
has in place to guard against company data being leaked to people outside
the organisation."

....

....

Return to page 67 of the Student's Book.

Reflection

How do you feel about the process of creating your troubleshooter? Is there anything you are particularly pleased with?

....

....

Is there anything you think is missing, or have you found any paths in the troubleshooter that you don't have answers for?

....

....

Homework

Create a poster to put on the classroom wall advising people about how to protect their computers from malware.

Chapter 4.4 Unauthorised access

Task A. Simulate a firewall

Fill in the table as you do the role-play exercise and record the results for each example.

Tip Note that some of the lines will not be needed as the access will be blocked.

For each example, state the outcome, either ALLOWED or BLOCKED. If it is blocked then give a reason.

Task	Result
Access the website at 192.168.3.76 port 443 from inside the trusted network	Direction: .... Destination: .... Port: .... Action: .... Direction: .... Destination: .... Port: .... Action: .... Result: ....
Access the website at 43.98.2.154 port 80 from inside the trusted network	Direction: .... Destination: .... Port: .... Action: .... Direction: .... Destination: .... Port: .... Action: .... Result: ....

Task	Result
Open a connection from the internet to port 22 on the trusted network	Direction: .... Destination: .... Port: .... Action: .... Direction: .... Destination: .... Port: .... Action: .... Result: ....
Open a connection from inside the trusted network to 64.63.2.21 port 22 on the internet	Direction: .... Destination: .... Port: .... Action: .... Direction: .... Destination: .... Port: .... Action: .... Result: ....
Open a connection from inside the trusted network to 64.63.2.21 port 300 on the internet	Direction: .... Destination: .... Port: .... Action: .... Direction: .... Destination: .... Port: .... Action: .... Result: ....

Return to page 69 of the Student's Book.

Task B. Keeping data safe inside a network

1 Would a firewall have been able to prevent this data from being leaked?

....

....

2 Should Faisal have had access to this data? Justify your answer.

....

....

3 How could file access permissions have helped avoid this situation becoming possible?

....

....

Return to page 71 of the Student's Book.

Reflection

Do you think it is better to be more or less strict when setting up security measures such as firewalls and file access permissions? Explain how you came to this conclusion.

....

....

....

....

Did your opinion on any of the topics covered during this lesson change at all because of what you learned? Explain your opinion.

....

....

Homework

Draw a cartoon that illustrates how a firewall works in multiple steps, like a comic strip. Make sure you explain what happens to both permitted traffic and blocked traffic when it reaches the firewall.

Chapter 4.5 Network connections and the IoT

Task A. Advantages and disadvantages of wired and wireless networks

Fill in the table to compare the advantages and disadvantages of wired and wireless networks. Make sure you think about the following aspects in your answer:

- Connection speed
- Security

	Advantages	Disadvantages
Wired network		
Wireless network		

Return to page 73 of the Student's Book.

Reflection

What IoT devices do you use at home? If you don't use any, what devices can be found in a typical home around the world?

....

....

Did you or your family take any security precautions when choosing or installing your device? What were they? If not, what security precautions do you think might be sensible?

....

....

Do you think that the benefit of having internet connected devices in a household is outweighed by the security risk? Explain and justify your answer.

....

....

....

Homework

Research a case study concerning a security issue with an IoT device. Find out what the security issue was, what happened as a result and how it was resolved.

Describe the security issue – when did it happen, and which device did it affect?

....

....

What happened as a result?

....

....

How was the issue resolved?

....

....

Chapter 4.6 Troubleshooter

Task A. Test the troubleshooter

Note down the advice given by your or your partner's troubleshooting tool for each scenario. In the rightmost column, evaluate the advice you were given. Was it correct? If it was not correct, where did the troubleshooting tool go wrong?

Scenario	Advice given	Evaluation
1		
2		
3		
4		
5		

Return to page 75 of the Student's Book.

Reflection

What do you think was the most successful thing about your troubleshooter?

....

....

What did you admire about your partner's project?

....

....

What do you think you could have improved on if you started the project again?

....

....

Homework

Create a troubleshooter for a specific IoT device of your choice.

Name of device: ....

Assessment checklist

- ☐ I can create a troubleshooting tool.
- ☐ I can test a troubleshooter.
- ☐ I can use a flowchart to identify different parts.
- ☐ I can resolve problems arising from creating a throubleshooter using features of the operating system.
- ☐ I can identify operating systems and what tasks they perform.
- ☐ I can identify the purpose of utility programs.
- ☐ I know how to simulate a firewall and protect a network from threats.
- ☐ I can keep data safe inside a network.
- ☐ I know the roles of ROM and RAM in my computer.
- ☐ I can list the benefits of IoT devices.
- ☐ I know the advantages and disadvantages of wired and wireless networks.

Chapter 5   Create with code 2

Project: Animal quiz

Chapter 5.1 Data types

Task A. What type of data?

Look at the piece of code below, then answer the questions.

```
1    name = input("Enter the player's name: ")
2    points = input("Enter how many points this
     player scored: ")
3
4    points = int(points)
5    triple_points_day = True
6
7    if triple_points_day:
8        print(name + " scored " + str(points) * 3 +
         " points!")
9    else:
10       print(name + " scored " + str(points) + "
         points!")
```

1 What is the data type of the variable name on line 1? ....

2 What is the data type of the variable points on line 2? ....

3 What is the data type of the variable points on line 4? ....

4 What is the data type of the variable triple_points_day on line 5? ....

5 What data type is the variable points cast to on line 10, and why? ....

6 This program will run, but the code contains a mistake. Which line has a mistake, and how should you fix it? ....

7 If the player's name is Kofi, and he scored 4 points, what would be the output after the code has been fixed? ....

Key terms

Boolean – a type of data that can have one of two possible values: true or false

Cast – change the data type of a piece of data

Condition – a test in a program that evaluates to a Boolean value – either true or false

Comparison operator – an operator that allows you to compare two values, for example to check whether they are equal, or one is greater than the other

Flow of control – the order in which the statements in a program are executed

Indentation – positioning code further in from the left

Logical operator – AND, OR or NOT

Logic gate – a circuit inside a computer that allows Boolean logic to be applied to one or more inputs

Program logic – how the design of the program is implemented

Pseudocode – a method of planning a program using statements that have a clear and precise meaning, but are not written in any particular programming language

Selection – when a program executes different code based on a condition

Sequence – statements in code that execute in the order they are written

Syntax – the structure of a statement in a programming language

Truth table – a diagram showing all possible combinations of inputs and outputs from a Boolean expression

Return to page 80 of the Student's Book.

Task B. Chatbot questions

Write down three questions that your chatbot could ask. An example has been provided to show you.

(Return to page 80 of the Student's Book.)

Question
What is your favourite sport?

Reflection

How confident are you that you could explain to another person what 'concatenation' means?

....

Which parts of this lesson did you remember learning about before?

....

....

Reflect on your work during this lesson. What are you most proud of?

....

....

....

Homework

Recap quiz

1 Give an example of each of these data types, as they would look in a Python program:

Integer ....   Boolean ....

String ....   Real ....

2 Write a line of Python code that would cast the variable `amount` to an integer .

....

3 Explain what is meant by casting.

....

....

4 Give an example of a situation when you might need to cast a variable in Python.

....

....

Chapter 5.2 Pseudocode

Task A. Similarities and differences

Annotate the flowchart and the pseudocode to describe the similarities and differences.

Flowchart

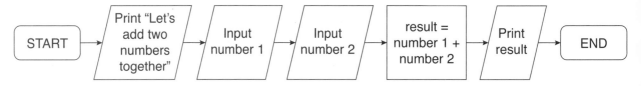

Pseudocode

```
OUTPUT "Let's add two numbers together"
number1 = INPUT number 1
number2 = INPUT number 2
result = number1 + number2
OUTPUT "The result is " + result
```

Return to page 81 of the Student's Book.

Task B. Flowchart to pseudocode

Translate the flowchart into pseudocode. Use the example in the Student's Book page 81 to help you.

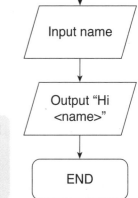

Figure 5.2.1 A simple sequence flowchart.

Return to page 82 of the Student's Book.

Task C. Pseudocode guidelines

Write some guidelines that you should follow when you are writing pseudocode. A suggestion has been given to start you off.

- Use capital letters for keywords, e.g. OUTPUT, INPUT.

- ....

- ....

- ....

- ....

- ....

Return to page 82 of the Student's Book.

Reflection

What do you think is important to remember when you are planning a program using pseudocode?

....

....

Did you find anything about using pseudocode difficult?

....

....

What did you learn when you tried to implement your partner's pseudocode?

....

....

Homework

Look at the different examples of pseudocode and evaluate each one. Is the pseudocode clear, precise and easy to understand? If not, what is wrong?

`Type in the numbers`
`Add up the first and second number`
`Add up the third and fourth number`
`Multiply them together`
`Print the result`	

`OUTPUT "Please type in a fruit"`
`INPUT fruit`
`OUTPUT "Please type in another fruit"`
`INPUT fruit`	

`OUTPUT "Enter a number"`
`result = calculate the number squared`
`OUTPUT "Your number squared is " + result`	

Chapter 5.3 IF, ELIF and ELSE

Task A. Write some conditions

Write some more examples of conditions – remember that the answer has to be either true or false. An example is given for you.

• I have finished my homework.

• ....

• ....

• ....

• ....

• ....

Return to page 84 of the Student's Book.

Task B. Evaluate the conditions

Evaluate each condition – is it true or false? Assume that the variable num has a value of 2.

1 5 > 0

2 8 == 9

3 8 != 9

4 4 <= 4

5 num < 7

6 num == True

Return to page 84 of the Student's Book.

Reflection

Was there anything you wanted to do with your chatbot but did not know how?

....

....

How would you find out how to do something you are stuck on in a Python program?

....

....

Homework

Write down the output of the program with the inputs specified.

```python
score = int(input("What was your test score? "))
if score > 50:
    print("Pretty good!")
elif score > 90:
    print("You're AMAZING")
else:
    print("Well done")
```

1 Input = 40 ....

2 Input = 51 ....

3 Input = 99 ....

Chapter 5.4 AND, OR, NOT

Task A. Recap logic gates

Label the following logic gates with the logical operator they represent, and a description of what the gate does. Choose the correct answers from the box. They are not in the correct order.

NOT	OR	AND
Either or both inputs are true		
Both inputs are true		
The input is false		

Gate			
Operator			
The output is true when...			

Return to page 87 of the Student's Book.

Task B. Complete the truth tables

Using the logic gate simulator program provided by your teacher, set up simulations of the logic gates AND and OR.

1 Complete the truth table for the AND gate. The inputs are A and B.

A	B	Output
1	1	
	0	0
0	1	0
0	0	

2 Write in words: When does an AND gate have an output of True (1)?

....

3 Fill in the truth table for the OR gate. The inputs are A and B.

A	B	Output
1	1	
1	0	
	1	
0	0	

4 Write in words: When does an OR gate have an output of True (1)?

....

Return to page 88 of the Student's Book.

Reflection

Do you prefer using true/false, on/off or 1/0 for Boolean values? Why?

....

....

What did you find difficult during this lesson? How did you overcome
your difficulties?

....

....

Homework

Look at this logic diagram which, uses two logic gates joined together. You can use
the logic gate simulator to help you with this task if you wish.

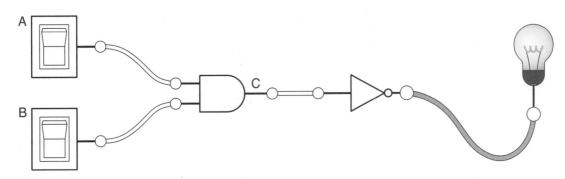

Figure 5.4.4 A logic gate diagram with two inputs and two gates.

1 Write down all the possible combinations of inputs A and B in the table.

A	B	C	Output

2 For each row, look at A and B, and work out what the output at C would be for
that combination. Write your answers in the table.

3 Finally, using the value you worked out for C as the input to the NOT gate, write
down the output for each row.

4 Write in words: When is the output for this circuit True (1)?

....

....

Chapter 5.5 Design and build a quiz program

Task A. Finish the pseudocode

Finish the pseudocode by adding more code to *input* and *check* the answer to this quiz question. The correct answers are A and B. Make sure your pseudocode is clear by using correct indentation.

```
OUTPUT "Which two animals have wings?"
OUTPUT "A – Bat"
OUTPUT "B – Parrot"
OUTPUT "C – Rhinoceros"
OUTPUT "D – Tiger"
```

Return to page 91 of the Student's Book.

Task B. Plan your quiz questions

Plan the text for the multiple-choice questions for your quiz. Each question should require at least one logical operator to check the answer, and you should try to include answers that require all three logical operators, AND, OR and NOT.

	Question	Answer
1		
2		
3		
4		
5		
6		
7		
8		

Return to page 92 of the Student's Book.

Reflection

Did it help you to plan how to check the answer to one question in pseudocode before you started writing in Python? Why, or why not?

....

What method do you think works best for you when planning a program?

....

....

Homework

Look at the Python code and label:

- code in a sequence
- a selection statement
- a conditional operator
- a logical operator
- a condition
- indentation.

```python
amount = float(input("Enter the price: "))
method = input("Would you like to pay with cash or card?")
discount = input("Do you have a staff discount? Y/N")
if discount == "Y":
    amount = amount * 0.8

if method == "card" and amount > 5:
    pin = input("Please type in your PIN")
else:
    print("Please pay " + str(amount) + " in cash")
```

Chapter 5.6 Showcase your quiz

Task A. Quiz time

Play the quizzes produced by the other members of your group, and record your score on the quiz as well as any notes you might need to give feedback later.

Who made the quiz?	Notes	My score

Return to page 93 of the Student's Book.

Reflection

What could you have done to make the process of creating your quiz easier?

....

....

What did you admire in another student's quiz?

....

....

How well do you think you met the project brief?

....

....

....

Homework

Look at the Venn diagrams. Use a logical operator (AND, OR, NOT) to write down what is represented by the shaded area in terms of A and B.

1

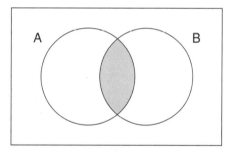

Answer: A .... B

2

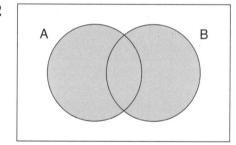

Answer: A .... B

3

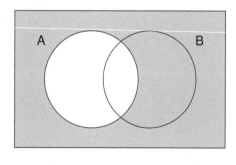

Answer: ....

4 Shade the diagram to represent NOT B

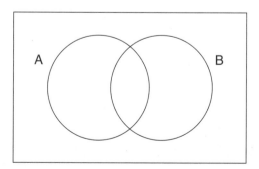

Assessment checklist

- ☐ I can write code to input and output data in Python.
- ☐ I can give an example of string, integer, real and Boolean data.
- ☐ I can convert variables between different data types in Python.
- ☐ I can round real numbers to a given number of decimal places in Python.
- ☐ I can follow a program in sequence in pseudocode.
- ☐ I can translate a flowchart to pseudocode.
- ☐ I can translate pseudocode to Python code.
- ☐ I know what the purpose of pseudocode is.
- ☐ I can follow selection statements in pseudocode.
- ☐ I can write a Python program using if, elif and else.
- ☐ I can identify a condition in a program.
- ☐ I can list the comparison operators.
- ☐ I can draw a truth table for a logic gate AND, OR or NOT.
- ☐ I can plan a program that uses selection in pseudocode.
- ☐ I know why indentation is important in pseudocode.
- ☐ I can modify starter code in Python to make a program.
- ☐ I can use logical operators AND, OR and NOT in a Python program.
- ☐ I can give helpful feedback to another student.

Chapter 6 Connect the world

Project: Virtual pen pal

Chapter 6.1 Binary and denary

Task A. Binary to denary conversion

Convert the following numbers from binary to denary using the method shown in the Student's Book page 98 . For all calculations, show your working.

1 11111

2 01100

3 10001

4 11010

5 111

Return to page 98 of the Student's Book.

Task B. Denary to binary conversion

Convert the following numbers from denary to binary using the method shown in the Student's Book pages 98 and 99 . For all calculations, show your working.

1 2

2 18

3 23

4 30

5 4

Return to page 99 of the Student's Book.

Key terms

ASCII – American Standard Code for Information Interchange, wildly used character encoding standard that represents characters in computers.

Binary – a number system that represents numbers using only two values: 0 and 1

Bit – a single **b**inary dig**it**, either 0 or 1

Compression – using an algorithm to reduce the size of a file

Copper cable – a type of cable that uses copper wire to transmit an electrical signal

Denary – the familiar base-10 number system, which uses the digits 0–9

Echo check – a test to see whether data has been transmitted correctly, which repeats the data back to the sender and checks for differences

Fibre optic cable – a type of cable that uses flexible glass fibres to transmit data as pulses of light

Instant message – a short text-based message that is delivered immediately, allowing them to be used for a real-time conversation

Interference – disruption or alteration to an electrical signal

LAN – Local Area Network, a network that connects devices in one physical location, for example a school or an office

Live stream – to broadcast an online event as it happens; for example, someone playing a video game, or presenting to the camera

PAN – Personal Area Network, a network that connects the devices within range of one person

Place value – the value that a digit has because of its position ('place') in the number

Reflection

Did you know anything about different number bases (base 10, base 2 etc.) before the lesson? Where did you learn this?

....

....

Why do you think you are learning about binary? Will it be important for you in the future?

....

....

....

Homework

Convert the following numbers between bases.

If the number has subscript $_{10}$ it means that the number is in denary and you need to convert it to binary.

If the number has subscript $_2$ it means that the number is in binary and you need to convert it to denary.

For all calculations, show your working.

1 84_{10}

2 10_{10}

3 10_2

4 11110100_2

5 255_{10}

6 00001011_2

7 100_{10}

8 1000_2

9 39_{10}

10 100101_2

Chapter 6.2 How are we connected?

Task A. Copper and fibre optic cables

1 Label each feature of these cables, and explain its purpose.

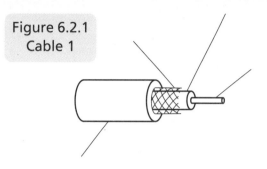

Figure 6.2.1
Cable 1

Figure 6.2.2
Cable 2

Type of cable:

....

....

Type of cable:

....

....

2 Note down the advantages and disadvantages of each type of cable.

Use the notes on Student's Book pages 102 and 103 to help you.

	Advantages	Disadvantages
Copper cable		
Fibre optic cable		

> Return to page 103 of the Student's Book.

Task B. PAN, LAN or WAN?

Read each statement and decide which size of network (PAN, LAN or WAN) it applies to. Tick the correct boxes to show your answer. You can tick more than one box per statement if necessary.

Statement	PAN	LAN	WAN
Connects devices over a large geographical area			
Connects devices in a small geographical area			
Formed by connecting together multiple local area networks			
Allows you to communicate across continents			
An example is a network owned by a business			
An example is the internet			
Connects multiple different devices			
Used to connect a wireless mouse to your laptop			

> Return to page 104 of the Student's Book.

Reflection

How could you use what you have learned about cables and sizes of network outside of this lesson?

....

....

What type of cables do you think connect your home or your school to the internet? How would you be able to find out?

....

....

What do you think you did really well in this lesson?

....

....

Homework

Draw a network or networks you are connected to. Explain the type of network and the devices that are connected to the network.

Chapter 6.3 ASCII

Reflection

How successful was your communication with your group? What do you think made it successful or unsuccessful?

....

....

....

What would you do differently if you did this exercise again?

....

....

Return to page 105 of the Student's Book.

Task A. Write your name using ASCII

1 Write out each letter in your name (continue into the second letter column if needed).

2 Use the ASCII table on the worksheet to look up the value of each letter in denary.

3 Convert the denary value to an **8-bit** binary value.

Tip	Make sure you have looked up the correct value – uppercase letters have different values to lowercase.

Letter	Denary	Binary	Letter	Denary	Binary

Return to page 105 of the Student's Book.

Homework

Can you work out the secret message written in ASCII?

ASCII code	Denary	Letter	ASCII code	Denary	Letter
0101 0111			0110 0100		
0110 0101			0110 1111		
0110 1100			0110 1110		
0110 1100			0110 0101		
0010 0000			0010 1110		

Message: ....

Chapter 6.4 Online communication

Task A. Choose and justify a communication method

For each scenario, choose an appropriate communication method to use, and give the reasons why you chose this particular method.

1 You are the owner of a small company and you want to tell your customers about a special offer that you are currently running.

....

....

....

2 You are a doctor and you need to give some advice to an elderly patient about some exercises they can do to help with a painful shoulder.

....

....

....

3 You are the leader of a group of people who play an online game that requires quick actions and coordination between many people.

....

....

....

Return to page 109 of the Student's Book.

Reflection

What is your preferred method of online communication? Does it vary depending on who you need to communicate with, and if so, how?

....

....

....

Homework

Explain the differences between online and offline communication methods in each of the categories. The first row has been filled in for you as an example.

	Online	Offline
Speed	• Happens instantly • Speed is the same regardless of the person's physical location	• Can communicate instantly but only if the person is in the same physical location
Sharing complicated information		
Miscommunication		
Cost		

Chapter 6.5 Data transmission

Task A. What was the message?

Write down the message you received from your partner, so you can echo it back.

....

....

....

Return to page 111 of the Student's Book.

Task B. Run-length encoding

Use run-length encoding to encode your message from Task A.

....

....

....

Use this space to write down the transmitted message from your partner.

....

....

....

Return to page 111 of the Student's Book.

Task C. Decode the message

Choose a colour for each letter in the message and record the letter and its colour in the key on the right-hand side. Starting from the top left square, colour in each of the boxes to make a picture.

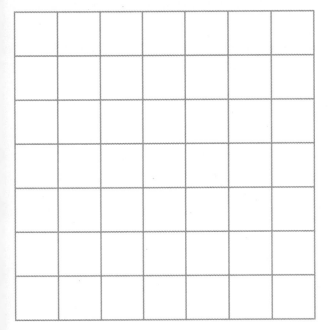 

Return to page 112 of the Student's Book.

Reflection

What was the most interesting part of the lesson today and why did it interest you?

....

....

How well do you think you worked with your partner? Did you have any problems working together today?

....

....

Homework

1 Colour your own pixel picture in the grid below, using a maximum of five different colours.

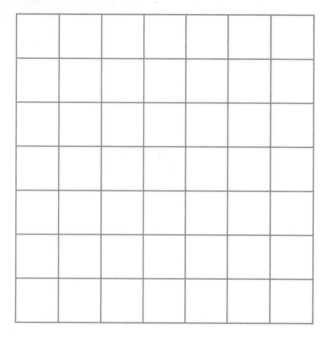 

2 Write down the run-length encoding for your picture.

....

....

....

Chapter 6.6 Finish your booklet

Task A. Feedback

Swap booklets and workbooks with a partner. **Your partner** should evaluate your booklet.

1 Tick the statements that have been covered successfully in this booklet:

- ☐ Convert a number from binary to denary.
- ☐ Convert 8-bit numbers between binary and denary.
- ☐ Explain why computers use binary to transmit data.
- ☐ Explain what materials are inside copper and fibre optic cables.
- ☐ Explain what interference is.
- ☐ Explain how interference affects data being sent via a cable.
- ☐ Explain the difference between PAN, LAN and WAN.
- ☐ Demonstrate how to write a word using ASCII.
- ☐ Convert ASCII codes back to letters and other characters.
- ☐ Describe the benefits and limitations of *at least one* method of online communication.
- ☐ Describe an echo check, and explain why it is used by a computer.
- ☐ Explain the word 'compression'.
- ☐ Use run-length encoding to compress some data.
- ☐ Decompress some data that has been run-length encoded.

2 What did you like about the booklet, and why?

....

....

....

3 What did you think could be improved in the booklet, and why?

....

....

....

When you have finished this task, swap back and read your peer feedback.

Return to page 113 of the Student's Book.

Reflection

What was the most useful thing you learned during this chapter?

....

....

How will you use what you have learned outside this subject?

....

....

How well do you think the project booklet you created met the brief? Were there any bits you didn't meet, and if so, why?

....

....

....

Homework

Draw a picture that includes as many things as possible that you have learned during this chapter.

Assessment checklist

- [ ] I can convert a number from denary to binary.
- [ ] I can convert a number from binary to denary.
- [ ] I can convert 8-bit numbers between binary and denary.
- [ ] I know why computers use binary to transmit data.
- [ ] I know how to work out the largest number that can be represented with a given number of bits.
- [ ] I know what materials are inside copper and fibre optic cables.
- [ ] I know what interference is, and the effect it has on data being sent via a cable.
- [ ] I know the difference between PAN, LAN and WAN.
- [ ] I know what types of network I am a part of.
- [ ] I can write a word using ASCII.
- [ ] I can convert ASCII codes back to letters and other characters.
- [ ] I understand why it is important to agree a set of rules for communication.
- [ ] I can describe the benefits and limitations of multiple methods of online communication, for example email, social media and voice chat.
- [ ] I can simulate an echo check with a friend, and I know why it is used by a computer.
- [ ] I can define the word 'compression'.
- [ ] I can use run-length encoding to compress some data.
- [ ] I can decompress some data that has been run-length encoded.
- [ ] I understand why it isn't always possible to compress data.
- [ ] I can add page numbers, headings and a table of contents to make a document look professional.
- [ ] I can explain to someone else how it is possible for me to send a message that is delivered instantly to a friend in another country.

Chapter 7 — The power of data

Project: Library database

Chapter 7.1 Keeping records

Task A. Label the catalogue card

Label the different data recorded on this catalogue card.

Figure 7.1.1 Library catalogue card.

Return to page 118 of the Student's Book.

Reflection

Do you think you would have found it easy to use a library 100 years ago? Why, or why not?

....

....

Imagine you are an older person who is not used to using technology. How would you feel about technology being introduced in the library?

....

....

Return to page 118 of the Student's Book.

Key terms

Big Data – an extremely large amount of data, which might be used to train a machine learning model

Character – any single letter, number, space or punctuation mark

Checkbox – a form input that allows one or more choices to be made from a list of options

Database – an organised collection of data, usually stored on a computer

Dry run – simulate how an algorithm will run by tracing how the value of each variable changes

Form – a method of collecting specific data, often to be added to a database

Length check – an algorithm that checks that the length of the data typed in is within a range

Linear search – checks each item in a list in turn until the search item is found, or the end of the list is reached

Machine learning – an area of computer science that uses algorithms and data to create software that can improve its own performance

Presence check – checks whether a form field has been filled in

Primary key – an assigned field in a database table that contains data that is both unique and not empty for every record

Radio button – a form input that allows a single choice to be made from a list of options

Record – a piece of information written down in a permanent form, to be used for later reference

Task B. Compare library systems

Write notes in the table to compare a card catalogue system to a modern library database system.

Key terms

Searching algorithm – a method of finding a specific item in a list

Table – a collection of related data, stored as columns and rows

Text box – a form input that accepts string data

Trace table – records how the values of variables in an algorithm change as the steps of the algorithm are followed

Training – providing data to a machine learning algorithm so that it can recognise patterns in the data

Type check – checks that the data entered has the correct data type

Validation – data typed into a form is checked to see whether it is a sensible value

Theme	Card catalogue	Modern database
What data is collected about a book?		
How is the data about a book stored?		
How would you find a specific book?		
How would you borrow a book?		

Return to page 118 of the Student's Book.

Homework

What physical items would be required for each of the two library systems?

Card catalogue	Modern library database

Chapter 7.2: Linear search

Task A. Describe a linear search in words

After watching the demonstration, describe how a linear search works.

Return to page 119 of the Student's Book.

Task B. Answer the questions about the trace table

Answer these questions about the linear search algorithm and trace table from Student's Book page 120.

1 Why does `item` gain the value of 17 on the third row of the table?

....

....

2 Why is the condition false on the fourth row of the trace table?

....

3 Why did Nikesh skip in the code from line 7 back to line 3 part way through the table?

....

....

4 What happens after his program outputs "Found it"?

....

....

....

Return to page 120 of the Student's Book.

Task C. Record the new algorithm

Use this space to write down your new pseudocode algorithm, which outputs a message if the search item was not one of the items in the list.

Return to page 121 of the Student's Book.

Reflection

How well do you think you could explain a linear search to someone who has not studied it in class?

....

....

Would you use a linear search to find a book in a library? If not, what would you do instead?

....

....

Homework

Some books have been left in three piles in the library. Each different book has been given a letter from A to F. The librarian must do a linear search through the books to find the book they need.

Pile 1	A	B	C	D	E	F
Pile 2	F	E	D	C	B	A
Pile 3	A	F	B	E	C	D

Use the information about the three different piles to answer the following questions:

1 Which pile would allow the librarian to find book B using the fewest comparisons?

....

2 How many comparisons would she need to find book F in pile 1?

....

3 What is the largest number of comparisons needed to find book E in any of the piles?

....

4 The library has 26 different books lettered A–Z. What is the highest number of comparisons the librarian would need to do to find a specific book in a pile, if the pile contained exactly one copy of each different book?

....

Chapter 7.3: Data capture forms

Task A. Would it be accepted?

Look at the form input and the validation specified in the table. Circle each piece of data that would be *accepted* by the validation.

1

Input	Validation	Data				
Text box	Length check, greater than 5	cheese	five	20	romance	189560

2

Input	Validation	Data				
Radio buttons with labels 1–5	Presence check	2		1	b	6

3

Input	Validation	Data				
Text box	Type check – number	999	three	2	1.5	"eight"

Return to page 124 of the Student's Book.

Task B. Design a data capture form

Use this space to design a form to input data about new books.

Your form should:

- gather the following information about each book: title, author, year of publication, genre
- use an appropriate form input for each piece of information
- include at least one type check, length check and presence check.

Return to page 125 of the Student's Book.

Reflection

How useful was it to receive feedback on your initial form design?

....

....

Do you need to make any changes to your design as a result of the feedback?

....

....

....

Next time you are asked to give feedback, how could you improve the feedback you give to your partner?

....

....

Homework

Look at this digital data capture form.

- Label the form input types
- Suggest and annotate the type of validation you would use for each of the inputs

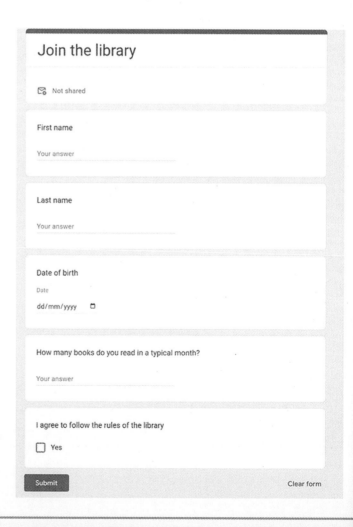

Chapter 7.4 Data validation

Task A. Draw and explain how you added data validation

For each type of validation, give an example of a field where you used it, and explain how you added the validation to that field and what criteria you used.

Presence check

Length check

Type check

Return to page 127 of the Student's Book.

Reflection

Did the validation you added catch any mistakes when you added the data for your books?

....

....

Which type of validation do you think is the most effective, and why?

....

....

Homework

If you make a mistake when entering data into a form that has validation, an error message is usually displayed. It is important to give a clear error message so that the person filling in the data understands what they have done wrong, and how to do it correctly the next time.

Look at the following validation rules and write a suitable error message to explain to the user how to input the data correctly.

Data	Validation rule	Error message
Year of publication	Type check: number	
Author	Presence check	
Title of book	Length check: >2	

Chapter 7.5 Recommend a book

Task A. Draw a mind map

Draw a mind map of the data you would need to collect to be able to recommend a book from your database to someone who comes to the library.

Return to page 128 of the Student's Book.

Reflection

Did you encounter any difficulties when working with your group to input your rating data?

....

....

How could you work better with other people the next time you are asked to work in a group?

....

....

Homework

Recommendation systems are used in lots of places; for example, when you buy something online you may be recommended other products that you may like, or if you watch a TV show on a streaming service, you may be asked to rate the show. Choose a recommendation system you have seen before. How do you think it works?

Chapter 7.6 Machine learning

Task A. Make a recommendation

Strategy 1

Who am I recommending a book for?	
Their highest rated book	
Genre of the book	
Recommendation (a book in the same genre)	

Strategy 2

Who am I recommending a book for?	
Their highest rated book	
Someone else who also read this book	
Recommendation (person B's highest rated book)	

Strategy 3

Who am I recommending a book for?	

Return to page 130 of the Student's Book.

Task B. Write a definition of machine learning

Use what you have learned this lesson to write a definition of machine learning.

....

....

....

....

Return to page 131 of the Student's Book.

Reflection

How do you feel about machine learning algorithms being used to recommend other books or products to you? Is it a good thing or a bad thing?

....

....

....

Are you happy for data about you, such as the ratings you give books or TV shows, to be used to train machine learning models? Why, or why not?

....

....

....

Is there any data about you that you would not want to be shared as part of a machine learning model?

....

....

Homework

Write up one of the book recommendations generated by your database to display in the library. Make sure the book you are recommending is one that you have read, so you can provide some detail about why the person may also like that book.

If you have read

...you might also like

This recommendation was generated by a database created by

Assessment checklist

☐ I can evaluate the advantages and disadvantages of a database, for example a card catalogue or a modern library database.

☐ I can use my research skills to find the information I need using a search engine.

☐ I can think about how another person may feel about modern technology.

☐ I can describe a linear search in words.

☐ I can follow the pseudocode for a linear search.

☐ I can trace the pseudocode for a linear search for a particular search item in a trace table.

☐ I can alter pseudocode to add features or correct errors.

☐ I know when to use a variety of form inputs.

☐ I can describe the following validation methods: presence check, type check and length check.

☐ I can design a data capture form using appropriate form inputs and validation.

☐ I can build a data capture form using appropriate software.

☐ I can add data validation to a form I have created in software.

☐ I can create a form that will collect and store the data I enter.

☐ I can work collaboratively with others to crowd-source data in a specific format.

☐ I can follow a specified strategy to make a book recommendation based on data.

☐ I can think of a new strategy combining data from multiple sources to make a book recommendation.

☐ I can define the term 'machine learning'.

☐ I know how machine learning might be used to make recommendations for TV shows I might want to watch, or products I might want to buy.

Chapter 8.1 Digital technology in the workplace

Task A. Mind map

Draw a mind map of the different uses of technology in the workplace you have been allocated.

Workplace:

....

Uses of technology in

....

Key terms

Artificial intelligence (AI) – the simulation of human intelligence by a machine

Automatic – the ability of a machine to perform a task without input from a human

Autonomous – the ability of a computer to perform a task without input from a human, but including the ability to react to circumstances as it finds them

Barcode – a series of stripes that contain data and can be scanned by a barcode reader device

Digital technology – any device or system that creates, stores or uses data

Event-driven programming – a style of programming where all code is written to respond to events, for example when a button is pressed

Fail – the expected outcome of the test does not happen

Invalid data – data that should *not* be accepted by a program

Pass – the expected outcome of the test happens when the test is performed

Radio Frequency Identification (RFID) tag – contains data that can be read via radio signal when the tag is close to a reader

Radio signal – a signal within a specific frequency band, used to transmit data

Trigger – cause to happen

Valid data – data that should be accepted by a program

Return to page 135 of the Student's Book.

Task B. Hardware devices in the workplace

Choose **two** different hardware devices used for input and/or output. For each device, explain what it would be used for in the workplace you have been focusing on.

Device 1

Hardware device: ....

Input or output device? ....

How the device is used

....

....

....

Device 2

Hardware device: ....

Input or output device? ....

How the device is used

....

....

....

Return to page 137 of the Student's Book.

Reflection

What sort of technology do you think you would like to use in your future job? Why does it interest you?

....

....

In what ways do you think the workplace will be different when you are older?

....

....

....

Homework

Ask an adult about the technology that is used in their workplace.

I asked .... who works at ....

What digital technology is used in your workplace?

....

....

....

....

How do you feel about using technology at work?

....

....

....

Chapter 8.2 Autonomous programming and AI

Task A. Is it autonomous?

Look at the descriptions of four different robotic systems below. Tick the correct boxes and use the final column to explain why you chose your answer.

Description	Automatic	Autonomous	Justify your answer
Parcel delivery drone			
Drink vending machine			
Machine that builds cars			
A robot vacuum cleaner			

Return to page 139 of the Student's Book.

Reflection

Was there anything you thought was true about automation before this lesson that you have now changed your mind about? What made you change your mind?

....

....

Return to page 139 of the Student's Book.

Task B. Automated or not?

Watch the presentations given by your classmates. Note down the different uses of technology in each workplace, and record whether you think each technology uses automation.

Workplace	Use of technology	Automation?	Notes

Workplace	Use of technology	Automation?	Notes

Workplace	Use of technology	Automation?	Notes

Workplace	Use of technology	Automation?	Notes

Return to page 139 of the Student's Book.

Homework

What uses of AI have you heard of?

....

....

....

Research a use of AI in the workplace. Note down what the technology does and how it helps the people working in that area.

AI technology I researched:

....

A workplace it is used in:

....

How is it used to help people in the workplace?

....

....

....

....

Chapter 8.3 Radio signals

Task A. Note down your ideas

Use this space to note down your ideas for possible workplace systems.

Return to page 143 of the Student's Book.

Task B. Design a system for use in the workplace

Our system will be used in ....

Describe briefly what the system does.

....

....

Write down a series of steps to describe how the system will work.

....

....

....

....

....

Return to page 143 of the Student's Book.

Reflection

How well do you think you worked with your partner during this lesson?

....

....

You will continue to work with your partner for the rest of this project. Write down two rules you want to stick to, so that you work well as a team.

1 ....

2 ....

Homework

Explain how radio signals are used in each of the following situations? You may need to do some research if you do not know the answers.

Situation	Explanation
Entering a railway platform	
Entering a building	
Borrowing a library book	

Chapter 8.4 Design a workplace system

Task A. Divide up the tasks

Look at the list of instructions you wrote in Task B on page 110. Write a list of tasks each micro:bit will need to be able to achieve. You may realise that you missed some tasks in your initial description, so you can add any extra tasks you think of now.

micro:bit 1	micro:bit 2

Return to page 144 of the Student's Book.

Task B. Write the pseudocode

Use this space to plan your program in pseudocode. You may need to use several different blocks of pseudocode depending on when your code will run. Give each block a heading; for example, "WHEN the program starts".

Return to page 145 of the Student's Book.

Task C. Dry run your pseudocode

Choose a test task which it should be possible to accomplish. Dry run your algorithm with the inputs required to complete that task and record the results.

What I am testing:

....

Test input:

....

Return to page 145 of the Student's Book.

Reflection

Did you spot any errors when you did your dry run? How useful do you think this process is?

....

....

Homework

Here is some code for the chef's micro:bit from the example scenario given in Lesson 3. Dry run the code using the inputs specified and write the missing answers in the shaded boxes.

```
1    WHEN the program starts:
2        SET order_number TO 0
3        SHOW square icon
4
5    WHEN button A IS PRESSED:
6        ADD 1 TO order_number
7        SHOW order_number
8
9    WHEN button B IS PRESSED:
10       RADIO SEND order_number
11       SHOW tick icon
```

What I am testing: Order number 1 can be transmitted from chef's micro:bit

Test input: A, B

Line	order_number	Input	Output	Radio
1				
2	0			
3				
		A		
5				
	1			
			1	
9				
10				
11			Tick icon	

Chapter 8.5 Test plans and test data

Task A. Create a test plan

Develop a test plan to test your program. Your test plan should include at least one test with invalid data.

#	Description	Input	Expected output	Result
1				
2				
3				
4				
5				

Return to page 147 of the Student's Book.

Reflection

Reflect on the two types of testing you have used during this lesson – dry runs and test plans.

Which type of testing did you prefer, and why?

....

....

In the future when you are asked to write a program, how will you test it? Do you think you will use either of these methods, or another way?

....

....

....

Homework

Look at the test plan, which has been written by a student. For each test, give a rating and, if necessary, explain what you would improve about the test.

#	Description	Input	Expected output
1	An order number can be transmitted by the chef	Press A to select the order number	The customer's micro:bit displays a smiley face
2	The customer micro:bit can be allocated a valid order number	Press A on the customer micro:bit 3 times to select order number 3	The number displayed changes with each button press, displaying 1, 2 and then 3
3	The customer micro:bit cannot be allocated an invalid order number	Press A on the customer micro:bit 10 times	The micro:bit does not display the number 10

Test 1

Comments

....

Test 2

Comments

....

Test 3

Comments

....

Chapter 8.6 Test your program

Reflection

Did you encounter any problems with the test plan? Describe the problem.

....

....

....

If you were asked to write a test plan again, what would you do differently?

....

....

Return to page 148 of the Student's Book.

Task A. Watch the demonstration

Watch the demonstration from another group, and note down how their system works.

Group we observed:

....

Workplace it is used in:

....

What does the system do?

....

....

Return to page 149 of the Student's Book.

Homework

Research an example of when a real-life system failed due to a software error.

Name of system:

....

What caused the system to fail?

....

....

What happened when the system failed?

....

....

Why do you think it is important that real-life systems are thoroughly tested?

....

....

Assessment checklist

☐ I can define the term 'digital technology'.

☐ I can explain how digital technology is used in a variety of workplaces.

☐ I can explain what a RFID tag is and how it works.

☐ I understand the difference between automatic and autonomous systems.

☐ I can explain how autonomous programming is used in robotics.

☐ I can write a program that uses two or more interacting physical devices.

☐ I can design a system using interacting devices, to be used in a workplace.

☐ I can plan an algorithm using pseudocode.

☐ I can plan pseudocode for an algorithm that happens when a particular event is triggered, such as pressing a button.

☐ I can dry run an algorithm with example input data.

☐ I can record the results of dry running an algorithm using a trace table.

☐ I know how to create a test plan.

☐ I can write tests using precise language.

☐ I know the difference between valid and invalid data.

☐ I can write a test to test an invalid input to a program.

☐ I can use a test plan to test a piece of software.

☐ I can use the results of testing to improve my program.

☐ I can give useful feedback about a system designed by someone else.